Usborne
History
of
Science
in
100 Pictures

Abigail Wheatley

Illustrated by Ian McNee

Designed by Samantha Barrett and Tom Lalonde

Science consultant: Christopher Parkin,
Museum of the History of Science, Oxford University

Internet Links

For links to websites with videos about famous scientists and their
discoveries, and more about key developments in science, from the
compass and electricity to vaccines and Dolly the Sheep, go to the
Usborne Quicklinks website at www.usborne.com/quicklinks
and type in the keywords 'history of science'.
Please follow the online safety guidelines at the Usborne Quicklinks website.

1

Early oar

This **ancient oar** was made by people who found food by hunting, fishing and gathering plants. They would have used the oar in a **canoe** made from a hollow log. Simple canoes were used all over the world and were probably the **first** invention for **transporting people**.

Ancient science

Even very early people experimented with the world around them, making tools and farming. Then, with the first civilizations, came counting, writing and more complex technologies for transportation and medicine.

Early farmers

2

This tool is a **sickle**, used by **early farmers** to harvest crops such as wheat. Between 12,000 and 2,000 years ago, people across the world learned how to farm plants and animals. This was such a huge leap forward, it's known as the **Agricultural Revolution**.

Bone sickle with stone blade

3

Ancient metalworking

Gold cow decorations, 4500BC

At around 6,500 years old, these cow decorations from Varna (now in Bulgaria) are some of the **oldest gold** objects ever found. People had only recently discovered how to extract **gold** and **copper** from rocks and to heat and hammer them to make ornaments and tools such as knives.

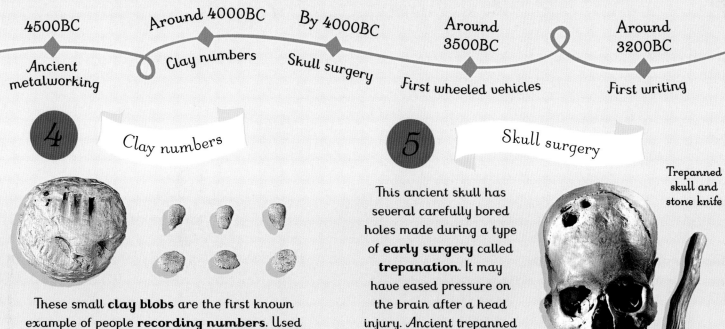

4 Clay numbers

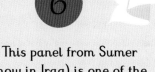

These small **clay blobs** are the first known example of people **recording numbers**. Used around 6,000 years ago in Uruk (now in Iraq), they represent things such as sheep owned by a particular person, and were stored inside the larger blob (which is hollow) to keep a **tally** of who owned what.

5 Skull surgery

This ancient skull has several carefully bored holes made during a type of **early surgery** called **trepanation**. It may have eased pressure on the brain after a head injury. Ancient trepanned skulls have been found all over the world.

Trepanned skull and stone knife

6 First wheeled vehicles

This panel from Sumer (now in Iraq) is one of the oldest scenes showing a **wheeled chariot** in use. Wheels were first used by armies in Sumer, around 5,500 years ago.

7 First writing

An example of **early writing**, this **clay tablet** from Kish (now in Iraq) dates from 3200BC. Writing was invented by many civilizations – in the Middle East, Egypt, China, Greece, India and Central America – by around 5,000 years ago. This invention helped people keep accurate **records** and share discoveries.

Around 2000BC
Water clock

1900BC
Early mathematics

1600BC
Sky disk

1200BC
Iron working

8 Water clock

This is an ancient Egyptian **water clock** - a pot with carefully positioned holes. When water was poured in, it gradually flowed out, and the falling water level showed **how much time** had passed. People in many different parts of the world invented similar clocks around the same time.

9 Early mathematics

This **clay disk** is inscribed with a **mathematical exercise** for students in Babylon (in the Middle East) to find out the area of the space between the triangles. Babylonians also used **mathematics** for things such as predicting the positions of the planets, and they were the first to divide an hour into 60 minutes.

10 Sky disk

This **bronze disk**, found in Germany, is inlaid with a gold Sun, Moon and stars. Dating from 3,600 years ago, it's the **oldest known image of the sky**. It may have been used for measuring the position of the Sun, to calculate the dates of midsummer and midwinter.

11 Iron working

This is a copy of an **early iron sword**. People in different parts of the world started working with iron around 3,200 years ago. Iron is harder than the metals that had previously been used, so **iron tools**, like this sword, were stronger and sharper than ever before.

2000BC - 212BC

460-370BC
The first doctors

384-322BC
Empiricism

287-212BC
First eureka moment

Hippocrates examining a patient

12 The first doctors

This carving shows ancient Greek doctor **Hippocrates**. Unlike most people who believed diseases were sent by gods, Hippocrates thought illnesses had natural causes. His followers became the **first professional doctors**, using treatments ranging from surgery to changes in diet.

13 Empiricism

Ancient Greek thinker **Aristotle** studied everything from physics to politics. He argued that **observation** and **experiment** are the only reliable ways to find things out. Now known as **empiricism**, this idea forms the basis of science today.

Portrait of Aristotle

14 First eureka moment

Ancient Greek crown similar to the one Archimedes tested

Eureka means 'I have found it!' and is used for **breakthrough moments**. Ancient Greek scientist **Archimedes** is supposed to have said it when getting in to his bathtub. He realized that when something is pushed underwater, it **displaces** the same **mass** of water as itself. He used a similar method to calculate the mass of a crown, proving it was not made of pure gold, but had some silver mixed into it.

EUREKA!!

5

279-194BC
Measuring the Earth

100BC
The first paper

80BC
Antikythera mechanism

0
An early compass

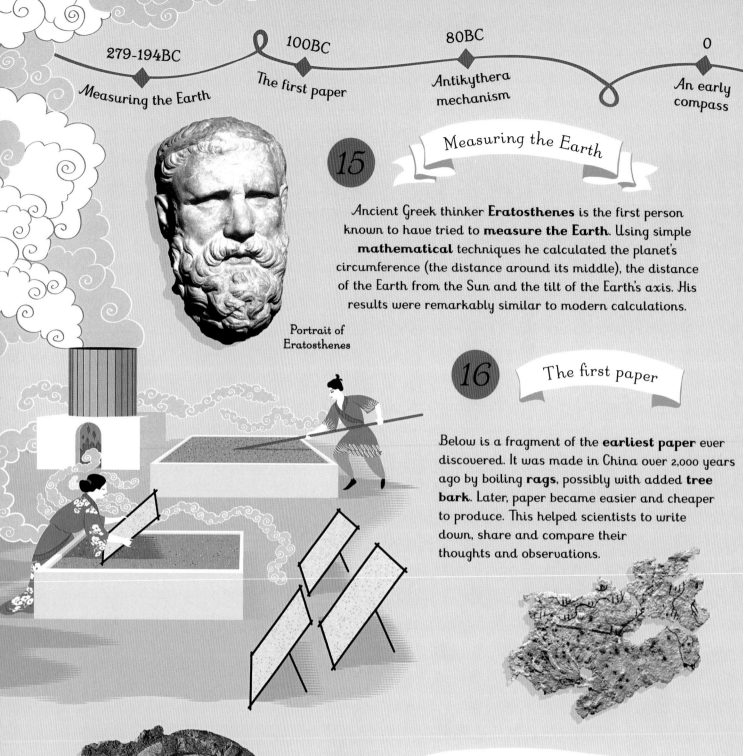

15 Measuring the Earth

Ancient Greek thinker **Eratosthenes** is the first person known to have tried to **measure the Earth**. Using simple **mathematical** techniques he calculated the planet's circumference (the distance around its middle), the distance of the Earth from the Sun and the tilt of the Earth's axis. His results were remarkably similar to modern calculations.

Portrait of Eratosthenes

16 The first paper

Below is a fragment of the **earliest paper** ever discovered. It was made in China over 2,000 years ago by boiling **rags**, possibly with added **tree bark**. Later, paper became easier and cheaper to produce. This helped scientists to write down, share and compare their thoughts and observations.

17 Antikythera mechanism

The **Antikythera mechanism**, found in a shipwreck, is an ancient Greek **machine** made of complex interlocking cogs. It was used for **predicting** the **movements of the planets** and solar eclipses and is sometimes described as the **first analogue computer**.

Part of the Antikythera mechanism

18 An early compass

This is a copy of an ancient Chinese **magnetic compass**. It was known as a 'south-pointing spoon' and was used for fortune-telling. The Chinese also had compasses to help them with **navigation**, probably made using naturally **magnetic stones**.

19 Armillary sphere

This is an **armillary sphere** – an instrument invented in both ancient Greece and China to calculate the **position of the Sun and stars** in relation to the Earth. This particular design was described by ancient Greek thinker **Ptolemy**. He thought the Sun revolved around the Earth – whereas in fact the Earth revolves around the Sun – but his armillary sphere would still have worked.

20 Mathematical martyr

Hypatia was a famous **mathematician** and thinker from Alexandria, Egypt, where she taught various subjects including **astronomy** (the study of stars and planets). She wielded a lot of influence, but it was a time of great change and upheaval, and she was killed by an angry mob. No one reallly knows why.

Statuette of Hypatia

The House of Wisdom

Painting made in Baghdad around 1237

This painting shows Muslim scholars **discussing ideas**. **Harun al Rashid**, a Muslim caliph (ruler) based in Baghdad around 800, encouraged scholars to debate, share and translate new and old books. This movement was known as the '**House of Wisdom**'.

The city of Baghdad

The Middle Ages

From around the year 800, powerful Muslim leaders in the Middle East and beyond presided over a golden age of science. Scientific advances were also made in Europe and China, too.

22 Alchemy

Muslim scholars, including **Al-Kindi** (shown here on the right), **Jabir ibn Hayyan** and **Muhammad ibn Zakariya al-Razi**, studied an area known as **alchemy**. They had unrealistic goals (such as creating life or making gold), but their rigorous **laboratory experiments** threw up important discoveries and paved the way for modern chemistry.

23 Astrolabe

This is an **astrolabe** – an instrument first invented in ancient Greece, but greatly improved and developed by **Muslim astronomers** from around 900. Astrolabes were used for many purposes including to **measure the position of the stars**, tell the time, and find north, south, east and west.

Astrolabe made in Syria around 900

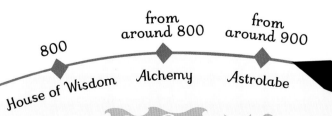

24 Early optics

This picture of an **eye** comes from an Islamic manuscript of the Middle Ages. One of the scholars who devoted his studies to **optics** (how eyes and light work) was **Ibn al-Haytham**, sometimes known as Alhazen. He showed that **light travels in straight lines**. He also realized that seeing is a result of light entering the eye – an idea that was revolutionary at the time.

Painting made in Baghdad before 1200

25 Father of medicine

This scene showing a **doctor** comes from **The Canon of Medicine**, a **medical book** written by **Ibn Sina**, known in the West as **Avicenna**. He is often proclaimed as the **father of modern medicine**, and his book was used regularly by doctors for the next 800 years.

26 Super star

European **astronomers** (like these ones) along with others from China, Japan, Iraq and Egypt, all left records that in the year 1006 they had seen a **new star**, so bright that it was visible even in the daytime. It was what's now known as a **supernova** – a massive explosion from a dying star. It's thought to have been the brightest star ever seen.

European astronomers in a painting from the Middle Ages

27 Early Earth science

The remains of ancient sea shells inspired **Shen Kuo**, a thinker from northern China. He had many new ideas, including about **how land formed**. Noticing sea shells preserved in rocks (**fossilized**) in an inland mountain, he realized that long ago, the shells had collected in mud on a sea bed, then turned to rock that gradually shifted until it formed land.

Fossilized sea shells

980-1037 — Father of medicine

1006 — Super star

1031-1095 — Early Earth science

1154 – 1440

1154
World map

Around 1230
Explaining the universe

After 1240
Circulation of the blood

1280s
First reading glasses

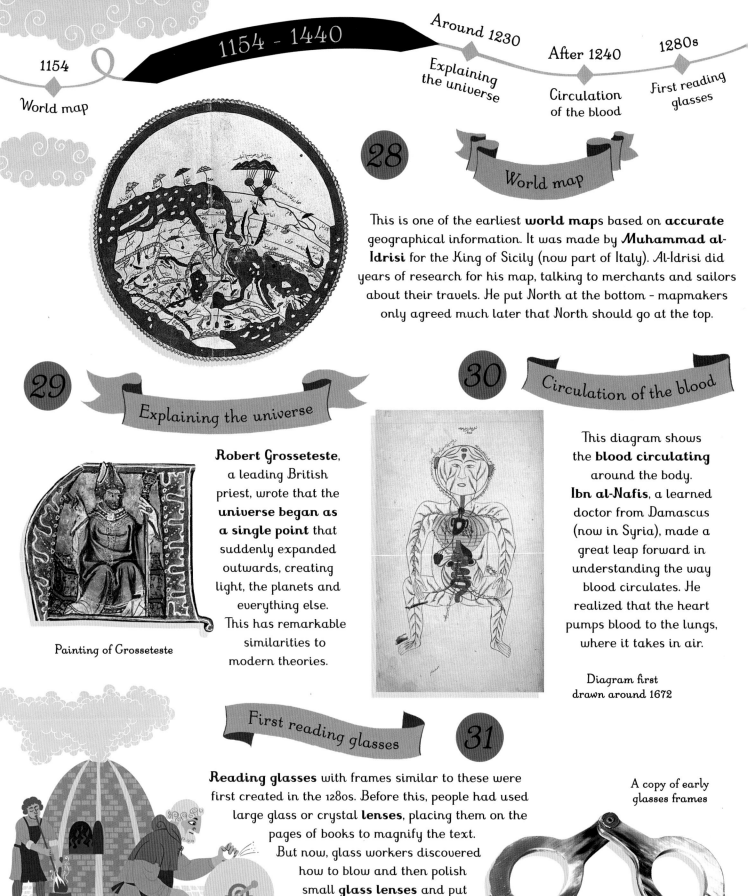

28

World map

This is one of the earliest **world maps** based on **accurate** geographical information. It was made by **Muhammad al-Idrisi** for the King of Sicily (now part of Italy). Al-Idrisi did years of research for his map, talking to merchants and sailors about their travels. He put North at the bottom - mapmakers only agreed much later that North should go at the top.

29

Explaining the universe

Robert Grosseteste, a leading British priest, wrote that the **universe began as a single point** that suddenly expanded outwards, creating light, the planets and everything else. This has remarkable similarities to modern theories.

Painting of Grosseteste

30

Circulation of the blood

This diagram shows the **blood circulating** around the body. **Ibn al-Nafis**, a learned doctor from Damascus (now in Syria), made a great leap forward in understanding the way blood circulates. He realized that the heart pumps blood to the lungs, where it takes in air.

Diagram first drawn around 1672

First reading glasses

31

Reading glasses with frames similar to these were first created in the 1280s. Before this, people had used large glass or crystal **lenses**, placing them on the pages of books to magnify the text. But now, glass workers discovered how to blow and then polish small **glass lenses** and put them in frames that perched on people's noses.

A copy of early glasses frames

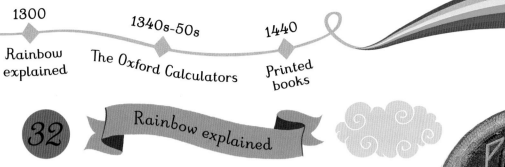

1300
Rainbow explained

1340s–50s
The Oxford Calculators

1440
Printed books

32 Rainbow explained

This painting shows a writer looking hard at a **rainbow**. Around the year 1300, two scholars, **Theodoric of Freiburg** (a German monk) and **Kamal al-Din al-Farisi** (a Persian scholar) both independently wrote down the correct explanation for **how rainbows are formed**. They realized that rays of light are bent when seen through raindrops, creating the rainbow effect.

A writer surrounded by a rainbow

A scholar measuring painted around 1350

33 The Oxford Calculators

Measuring things such as **heat and light** became possible for the first time thanks to a group of scholars known as the **Oxford Calcuators**. Based at the University of Oxford (in England) they used **mathematics** to tackle scientific problems that had puzzled experts for centuries.

34 Printed books

This **book**, one of the first to be **printed** in Europe, was made by **Johannes Gutenberg**. He created **movable type** – metal letter shapes that could be grouped together to print books quickly. Before this, books were copied by hand, or printed from hand-carved wooden blocks. Suddenly, books came down in price, so scientists could share ideas much more easily.

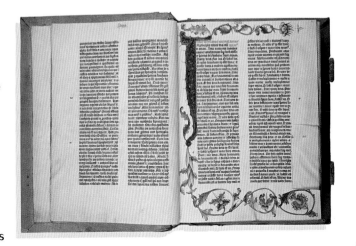

A printed book from 1455

Moving Earth

Copernicus's idea of how the planets move

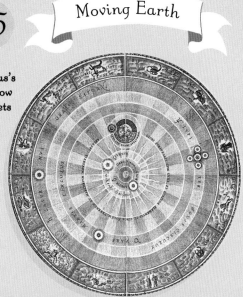

This diagram shows the **Earth** and other **planets moving around the Sun**. This revolutionary idea was put forward around 1514 by Polish scientist **Nicolaus Copernicus**. For centuries, since the time of Ptolemy, everyone believed that the Sun circled the Earth. Copernicus explained his idea to colleagues in 1514 but didn't publish it until 1543, as he knew how controversial it was.

36 Anatomy

Heart from an anatomy book of 1543

This drawing of a **human heart** by **Andreas Vesalius** was made by studying a dead body – a science known as **anatomy**. Anatomy dates back to ancient Greece, but was banned in the Middle Ages. From the 1540s, people began to study it again, publishing books with **detailed drawings** that led to many medical advances.

Enlightenment

Over the centuries, more and more people became fascinated by science. They started reading books about it, doing their own experiments and meeting to discuss scientific ideas.

37

Earth still moving

These **telecopes** were designed and used by **Galileo Galilei**, an Italian scientist. Based on his observations of the sky through these telescopes, Galileo argued that Copernicus had been right in suggesting that the **Earth** and other **planets move around the Sun**.

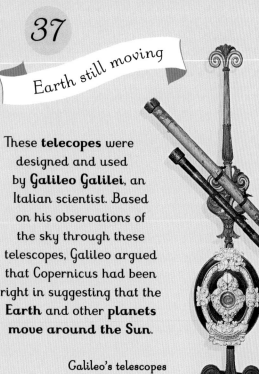

Galileo's telescopes on an elaborate stand

In 1633 the **Catholic Church** put Galileo on trial, saying his ideas went against the Bible. Galileo was forced to say he had changed his mind, but whispered 'Still, it moves!' as he left the court room, convinced that the Earth really does move around the Sun.

38 Microscopes

Early **microscopes**, like this one, were invented when scientists such as **Robert Hooke** realized that **lenses** already used in telescopes could be arranged to give a clear view of very small things. Now people could see the delicate, **microscopic structures** of things such as plant stems, lungs, blood and of tiny living creatures such as fleas.

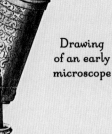

Drawing of an early microscope

Portrait of Isaac Newton

39 Gravity

Brilliant British scientist **Isaac Newton** was the first to describe **gravity**, a force that attracts small objects (such as apples) to big objects (such as the Earth). He is supposed to have come up with the idea when he watched an apple fall and wondered what made it drop down rather than up. He also helped to develop **mathematical** ways of explaining the way forces such as gravity work.

40 First scientific expedition

Maria Sybilla Merian, a German scientist, made this drawing while on the **first ever** official **scientific expedition**. She spent two years in Suriname, South America, making detailed drawings and studying the **life cycles** of the **insects** that lived there. She proved that they went through different stages, for example, from egg to caterpillar to butterfly.

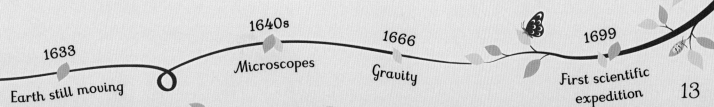

1633
Earth still moving

1640s
Microscopes

1666
Gravity

1699
First scientific expedition

Naming names

41

Carl Linnaeus was a Swedish scientist who developed a **system** that gave a **unique Latin name** to each living thing. This meant all scientists could be sure they were referring to the same plant or animal. Linnaeus' system is still used today.

Linnaeus writing in his garden

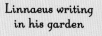

Marine chronometer

42

This is a **marine chronometer** - a type of clock invented for use on ocean voyages. Chronometers were invented because sailors needed to know the exact time to keep track of where they were, but couldn't use **traditional clocks** powered by swinging weights because the movement of the waves disrupted them.

Chronometer made in 1735

Electrical experiment

43

American thinker **Benjamin Franklin** wanted to show that **lightning** is a **form of electricity**, so the story goes that he took a kite and tied onto its tail a **Leyden jar** - an early device for storing electricity. His son then flew the kite in a storm. Sure enough, the kite collected electricity, which was stored in the Leyden jar. But it was an incredibly dangerous experiment and Franklin and his son could easily have died

A Leyden jar similar to the one Franklin used

1735
Naming names

Around 1735
Marine chronometer

1752
Electrical experiment

1772
Father of chemistry

Father of chemistry

French scientist, **Antoine Lavoisier,** was known as the **Father of Chemistry**. He used this glass jar while working to identify the simplest substances from which all other substances are made, such as **carbon** (identified in 1772) and **oxygen** (1779). They're known as **elements**. Lavoisier's discoveries laid the groundwork for all of modern chemistry.

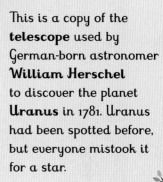

Jar used by Lavoisier for his chemistry experiments

Discovery of Uranus

This is a copy of the **telescope** used by German-born astronomer **William Herschel** to discover the planet **Uranus** in 1781. Uranus had been spotted before, but everyone mistook it for a star.

Copy of the telescope used to discover Uranus

First vaccination

British scientist **Edward Jenner** pioneered the **first vaccination.** He wanted to prove that having a mild disease called cowpox prevented people from getting smallpox, a killer disease. Using pus from cowpox swellings, Jenner deliberately infected a young boy with cowpox. Later, he infected the same boy with smallpox, but thankfully he remained well. **Vaccines** for other diseases soon followed.

Drawing of the cowpox swellings used by Jenner in the first vaccination

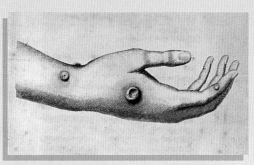

1735 - 1796

1781
Discovery of Uranus

1796
First vaccination

47 First battery

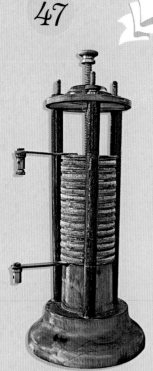

The **first battery** was invented by Italian scientist **Alessandro Volta**. He stacked circles of **copper** and **zinc**, separated by fabric soaked in salty water, and then connected the top and bottom with a wire. He found that **electricity** flowed through the stack and the wire. Lots of electrical inventions using batteries quickly followed.

Revolution

From around 1800, new discoveries from steam power to photography started a scientific revolution. Suddenly, science started changing the way ordinary people lived.

48 Electricity research

This equipment was used by British chemist **Michael Faraday** in intensive experiments to discover more about **electricity**. During this work he found ways to measure the amount of electricity flowing through different substances and invented a very simple type of **electric motor**.

49 Early computers

This is part of a **mechanical calculator** built from cogs and wheels by **Charles Babbage**. He called it the **Difference Engine** and also designed a bigger machine, the **Analytical Engine**, that could perform complex calculations when cards were slotted into it to tell it what to do. It was the **first programmable computer**. **Ada Lovelace**, another British mathematician, wrote the **first computer programs** for it. But Babbage only managed to build part of it, as it cost too much.

Part of Babbage's Difference Engine

1799 – 1839

1829

Early steam engines

around 1830

Chloroform

1839

Early photography

50 Dinosaurs discovered

This jaw and tooth come from of one of the **first dinosaurs** to be **identified scientifically**. Preserved in stone, or **fossilized**, these bones were studied by British scientists **William Buckland** and **William Conybeare**. They suggested they came from an ancient creature they named **Megalosaurus**, meaning 'huge lizard'. Soon remains of other dinosaurs were being discovered all over the world.

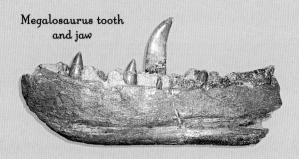

Megalosaurus tooth and jaw

Stephenson's Rocket

51 Early steam engines

The **Rocket** was a **steam engine** built in 1829 by **Robert Stephenson**. Although other inventors experimented with using steam to power engines that could **transport** people, Stephenson's design was the most impressive. The Rocket's design inspired a golden age of steam train travel over the next 150 years.

52 Chloroform

This bottle, containing a substance known as **chloroform** (discovered around 1830), changed medical history. One evening a doctor named **James Simpson** tried breathing some in. He lost consciousness but woke up the following morning, having proved that chloroform put people safely to sleep. Soon it was widely used to **relieve pain** during surgery or childbirth.

Dr. Simpson's chloroform bottle

53 Early photography

This **early camera**, designed by leading French inventor **Louis Daguerre**, was used to take an **early type of photograph**, known as a **Daguerreotype**. The camera used light-sensitive chemicals to capture an image on a metal plate.

A Daguerreotype camera

Evolution

54

This sketch by British naturalist **Charles Darwin** shows his big idea, which was known as **evolution by natural selection**. Darwin noticed some individuals with a feature - for example, birds with longer beaks - that gives then an advantage in competing for food and making them more likely to survive. He called this **natural selection**. Their offspring have longer beaks and survive better; longer beaks become more and more common, until eventually the whole species has them. Darwin called this **evolution**. This is still one of the most debated ideas in science.

55

Germ theory

Louis Pasteur, a French biologist, did pioneering work on **germs** - tiny organisms that cause **disease**. He was the first to prove that germs couldn't grow in containers that were completely clean, and realized that diseases spread when germs were passed from one place or person to another. Known as **germ theory**, this idea eventually saved countless lives.

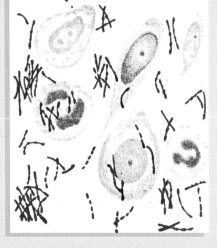

Early drawing of germs

Pea genes

56

These **peas** were used more than 150 years ago by Czech monk, **Gregor Mendel**, in his ground-breaking research on **genes**. Genes are the things that allow living creatures to pass on their own characteristics to their young. By breeding pea plants he proved that **parent** plants could pass on things such as stem length and seed shape to their offspring.

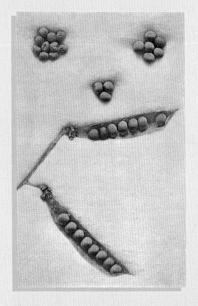

1859-1888

1876
First telephone

by 1879
First lightbulbs

1888
First car

57 Periodic Table

Russian scientist **Dmitri Mendeleev** studied **chemical elements** like the ones below, noting that despite differences, many had **similar properties**. He created a table, listing all known elements in order of their **atomic weight** (the mass of their atoms). This is known as the **Periodic Table**. Astonishingly, he found the elements fell naturally into groups with similar properties.

Metallic elements calcium, beryllium and magnesium

58 First telephone

Alexander Graham Bell was one of many scientists who experimented with designs for electric telephones. Bell's was the **first telephone** that worked well, and it even managed to impress the notoriously picky British monarch, Queen Victoria.

An early telephone designed by Bell

First lightbulbs

59

American inventor **Thomas Edison** designed and made this **electric lightbulb**. Many other inventors, including British scientist **Joseph Swan**, also designed lightbulbs around the same time. Despite fierce rivalry, in 1883 Swan and Edison set up a joint company to make and sell lightbulbs.

An early lightbulb

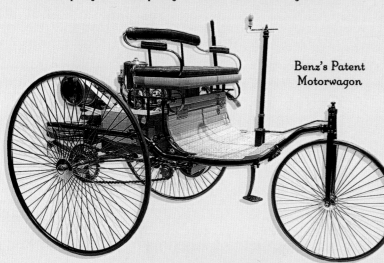

Benz's Patent Motorwagon

60 First car

The **Benz Patent Motorwagon** was the **first car** to be put on sale to the public. It was designed and built by German engineer **Karl Benz**. **Martha Benz**, his wife, drove the car on its first long-distance journey, creating huge public interest in the vehicle.

19

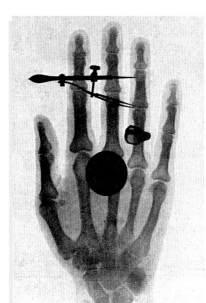

X-ray of a hand by Röntgen

61 X-rays discovered

This is one of the first ever **X-ray** photographs. It was taken by **Wilhelm Röntgen**, who discovered X-rays when passing **electricity** through a glass tube inside a box. When some chemical-coated paper at the other end of his lab glowed, he realized mysterious rays, which he called X-rays, were passing through the tube and box. He helped doctors use X-rays to see inside the human body.

62 Electrons discovered

This glass tube was used by **Joseph John Thomson**, who passed **electricity** through it, producing rays known as **cathode rays**. He realized they were formed of **particles smaller than atoms** – then the tiniest known things. These minute particles were in fact *parts* of atoms and were named **electrons**.

The Atomic age

Atoms are the tiny building blocks that make up the universe. As scientists started to understand them, all sorts of things became possible – from televisions to terrifying weapons.

63 Radioactivity

Marie Curie used this equipment when investigating a type of ray given off by substances found in rare rocks. She identified two new elements that gave off these rays and named them '**radium**' and '**polonium**'. She also invented a new word, '**radioactive**,' to describe them. Curie won two Nobel Prizes for her groundbreaking work.

1895
X-rays discovered

1897
Electrons discovered

1895 - 1913

First radio

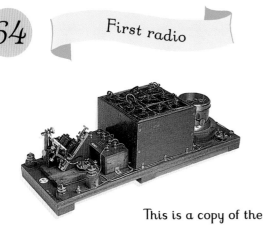

Model of the
Wright Flyer 1

This is a copy of the **first radio transmitter**. It was designed by Italian scientist **Guglielmo Marconi**, when experimenting with **radio waves**. His equipment successfully used radio waves to send signals through the air over long distances.

65

First plane flight

The **first successful plane flight** was made in 1903, in this plane, the **Wright Flyer 1**, designed by American brothers **Orville** and **Wilbur Wright**. Their plane flew for less than one minute, but this was enough to make history. Soon, more sophisticated planes were being designed and flown.

66

Continental drift

In 1911 a thoughtful German scientist, **Alfred Wegener**, proposed the idea of **continental drift**. He argued that the Earth's land masses move very, very slowly over the surface of the planet. At first other scientists dismissed this idea, but it's now an accepted fact.

Top map showing the Earth's land masses at the time of the dinosaurs

Lower maps showing how land masses have slowly separated over time

67

Model of atom

This model of the **atom** was agreed by scientists from around 1913. It shows **electrons** circling around a dense central area known as a **nucleus**. It was **Ernest Rutherford** (British) who showed atoms have a nucleus, while **Niels Bohr** (Danish) explained how electrons move around the nucleus.

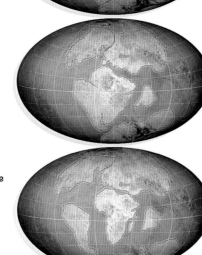

1898
Radioactivity

1900
First radio

1903
First plane flight

1911
Continental drift

1913
Model of atom

1915 — General relativity
1925 — Hydrogen Sun
1926 — First television
1928 — First antibiotic
1932 — Neutrons

Photo of Einstein

68 General relativity

Brilliant German physicist **Albert Einstein** put forward the theory of **general relativity** in 1915. He realized that Newton's idea of **gravity** didn't work for tiny things such as **atoms**, or vast things such as **planets**, that seemed to 'fall' in curves rather than straight lines. Einstein came up with the idea of *spacetime* – uniting time, height, width and depth. He argued that objects bend spacetime because of their gravity, creating curved paths to move along.

69 Hydrogen Sun

The **Sun** had puzzled scientists for years as they tried to find out what it was made of. Then, in 1925 **Cecilia Payne-Gaposchkin** showed that the Sun was mostly made of very light **gases** – some **helium** but mostly **hydrogen**. This helped scientists find out how stars form, and why they shine. That's because hydrogen **atoms** fuse together in a **nuclear reaction**, generating huge amounts of light and heat.

Image of the Sun showing a 'loop' of hydrogen and helium

70 First television

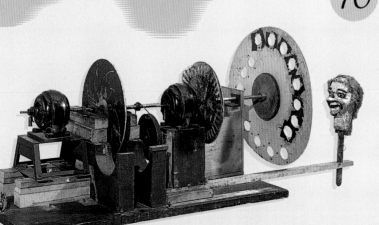

John Logie Baird built the **first** working **television transmitter**, using old boxes, needles and bicycle light lenses. He was the most successful of many scientists who experimented with equipment to transmit **moving pictures**. More sophisticated versions of Baird's invention were soon sending television pictures over long distances.

71 First antibiotic

It was in the dish shown here that **Alexander Fleming** accidentally discovered *penicillium* fungus, leading to the **first antibiotic**. Fleming was studying **bacteria** (infectious **germs**) but noticed that the penicillium stopped them from spreading. *Penicillin*, an **antibiotic medicine**, was developed from penicillium, curing many infectious diseases.

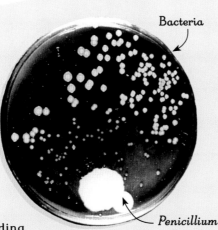

Bacteria

Penicillium fungus

72 Neutrons

This is the equipment used by **James Chadwick** to prove the existence of **neutrons** – tiny **particles** inside the **nucleus** of **atoms**. Chadwick bombarded these foil sheets with **alpha particles** (a type of **radioactivity**) and detected particles as they passed through the wax discs shown here.

73 First electronic computers

British computer scientist **Alan Turing** invented an electronic machine known as the *Bombe* during the Second World War (1939-1945). He used it to crack German codes created by other complex electronic machines. A British engineer named **Tommy Flowers** then developed Turing's technology to create *Colossus*, the **first** true **electronic computer**.

A copy of Turing's Bombe

74 Nuclear bombs

The first **nuclear explosions** were made by firing **neutrons** at **radioactive** materials to create a man-made **nuclear reaction**. Scientists found out how to use nuclear reactions to make light and heat, and deadly weapons. In 1945, two **nuclear bombs** were dropped on Japan. This helped to end the Second World War, but killed thousands of innocent men, women and children.

75 DNA

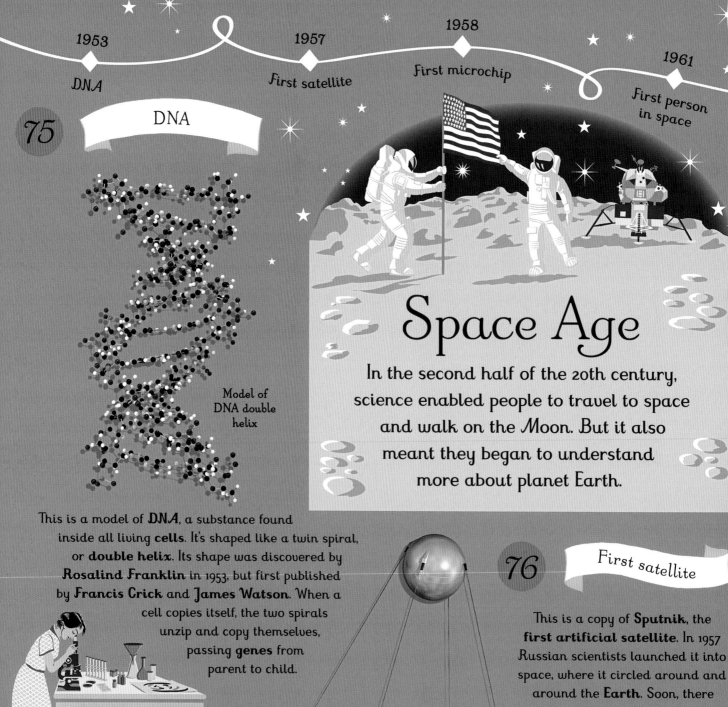

Model of DNA double helix

Space Age

In the second half of the 20th century, science enabled people to travel to space and walk on the Moon. But it also meant they began to understand more about planet Earth.

This is a model of **DNA**, a substance found inside all living **cells**. It's shaped like a twin spiral, or **double helix**. Its shape was discovered by **Rosalind Franklin** in 1953, but first published by **Francis Crick** and **James Watson**. When a cell copies itself, the two spirals unzip and copy themselves, passing **genes** from parent to child.

76 First satellite

This is a copy of **Sputnik**, the **first artificial satellite**. In 1957 Russian scientists launched it into space, where it circled around and around the **Earth**. Soon, there were more satellites, many used for tasks such as transmitting radio signals across the globe.

77 First microchip

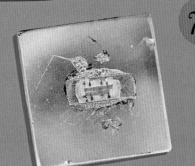

The **first ever microchip**, shown here, was created by American electrical engineer **Jack Kilby**. It has minute **electronic circuits** sealed onto a chip of **silicon**. Before this, electronic machines used slow, bulky electrical wires. The microchip made **computers** and other electronic machines much smaller and faster.

24

1953 - 1969

1962
Silent spring

1965
Plate tectonics

1969
Moon landing

78 — First person in space

Yuri Gagarin, born in Russia, was the **first person** to travel to **space**. Aboard spacecraft **Vostok 1**, he made one circuit around the **Earth**, lasting just over one a half hours, inspiring people all around the world.

Photo of Yuri Gagarin

79 — Silent Spring

American biologist **Rachel Carson** wrote a ground-breaking book, **Silent Spring**. It showed evidence that **chemicals** used to kill pests in fact killed many other animals, and even humans. Eventually, these chemicals were banned.

Photo of Rachel Carson

Plate tectonics — 80

This map shows that the **Earth**'s crust is divided into vast **plates** – an idea known as **plate tectonics**. In the 1960s scientists came to realize that each vast plate moves by sliding around very, very slowly over a layer of hot, molten rock thousands of miles underground.

Map of the Earth's plates

81 — Moon landing

In 1969 astronauts **Neil Armstrong** and **Buzz Aldrin** became the **first people to step onto the Moon**. After years of preparation and many test missions, the astronauts walked on the Moon as part of a historic mission, known as **Apollo 11**. Their moon walk was broadcast live on television to millions of people around the world.

82 MRI scanning

The first **MRI scan** was performed by **Raymond Damadian**, **Lawrence Minkoff** and **Michael Goldsmith** in New York state, U.S.A. It produced this image of a man's chest.

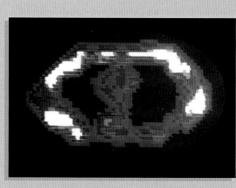

MRI stands for **magnetic resonance imaging**. Images from MRI scans can show soft parts inside the body, and are now a vital tool for doctors detecting diseases such as cancer.

Photo of Wangari Maathai

83 Green Belt Movement

Wangari Maathai, shown here, was a pioneering environmental activist, founding the **Green Belt Movement** after developers cut down trees, creating barren deserts where forests had once been in Kenya, Africa. Maathai organized thousands of people, many of them women, to collect seeds from remaining local trees, grow them in recycled containers, and then plant them, **restoring deforested areas** near their homes.

84 Voyager probes launched

This **probe**, or uncrewed spacecraft, is one of two launched into space in 1977 as part of the **Voyager program**. Both probes passed close to the planets **Jupiter**, **Saturn**, **Uranus** and **Neptune**, sending back the first pictures and information about their weather systems and moons. The probes then continued deep into space and are still sending back information today.

1977
MRI scanning

1977
Green Belt Movement

1977
Voyager probes launched

85 First full DNA genome

This is **phiX174**, the first organism to be given a **full DNA 'genome'** - a complete list of all its **genes**. British scientist **Fred Sanger** chose to work with phiX174 because it's a **virus** - a small, simple organism. The method Sanger used to extract and list its DNA was later used by other scientists to make a genome for bigger, more complex living things, including humans.

86 First IVF baby

Evening News
BRITAIN'S BIGGEST EVENING SALE
LATE SPECIAL CITY PRICES

Meet Louise, the world's first test-tube arrival

SUPERBABE

Wide-eyed Louise Brown pictured in hospital 18 hours after she was born. Today she's doing well. See Page Three

This photo shows **Louise Brown**, the first baby to be born through **IVF**, a technique developed for people unable to have babies naturally. British doctors **Patrick Steptoe** and **Robert Edwards** collected egg cells from Louise's mother and sperm cells from her father, and mixed them in a container. They then put an egg back into the mother's body. Nine months later, baby Louise was born.

87 Superstring theory

If you could see the **tiniest particles in the Universe**, they might look like this. According to '**superstring theory**', particles inside **atoms** are made up of even tinier particles like tiny, vibrating loops or '**strings**'. These are the smallest things there are, and come in pairs - one '**boson**' and one '**fermion**' - that balance each other. This idea was thought up to try to unite Newton's theory of **gravity** with Einstein's theory of **general relativity**, to make one theory that explains everything. But it's incredibly hard to prove.

An artist's idea of how 'strings' might look

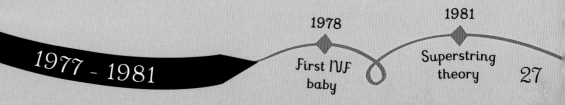

1977
First full DNA genome

1977 - 1981

1978
First IVF baby

1981
Superstring theory

27

88 — Genetic fingerprinting

This is the **first genetic fingerprint** – the unique pattern of **genes** in one person's **DNA**. Police now use genetic fingerprints to match suspects to DNA found at crime scenes and solve crimes.

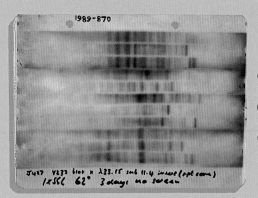

1989-870

Digital era

As the 20th century advanced, more powerful computers could process more information than ever before, enabling scientists to investigate minute particles and explore distant stars and planets.

World Wide Web — 89

British computer scientist **Tim Berners-Lee** used this computer to start the **World Wide Web**. He created **web pages** and **hyperlinked text** that could be clicked on to jump from one page to another, using the **internet**. His computer was the first ever '**web server**', used for storing and getting to web pages.

Hubble space telescope — 90

The **Hubble Space Telescope** took this picture of distant stars and gas. The telescope was launched into space in 1990 and is still sending amazing pictures back to Earth today.

1992
Exoplanets detected

1995
GPS fully functioning

1996
Dolly the sheep

1997
Mars Pathfinder

91 Exoplanets detected

In 1992 Polish astronomer **Aleksander Wolszczan** became the first to find evidence of exoplanets - planets outside the **Solar System** (the Sun and the planets near it). While studying signals from a telescope pointed at a distant star known as **PSR B1257+12**, he detected two exoplanets circling it. Since then, many more exoplanets have been found circling other stars.

Artist's impression of exoplanets circling a distant star

92 GPS fully functioning

This satellite is part of **GPS**, a network of **satellites** that **circles the Earth**, sending signals that help people find out exactly where they are. GPS became fully functional in 1995. Today, millions of people use it.

93 Dolly the sheep

Dolly was the **first large animal** ever to be **cloned** - she was grown from an ordinary body cell taken from another adult sheep. She lived to the age of six and a half.

Mars Pathfinder 94

This is a robot **rover** vehicle that reached **Mars** as part of the **Mars Pathfinder** project. The uncrewed Pathfinder spacecraft parachuted onto the surface of Mars in 1997. The rover drove out and started carrying out tests, sending more information than ever before to Earth from the red planet.

A model of a rover sent to Mars by Pathfinder

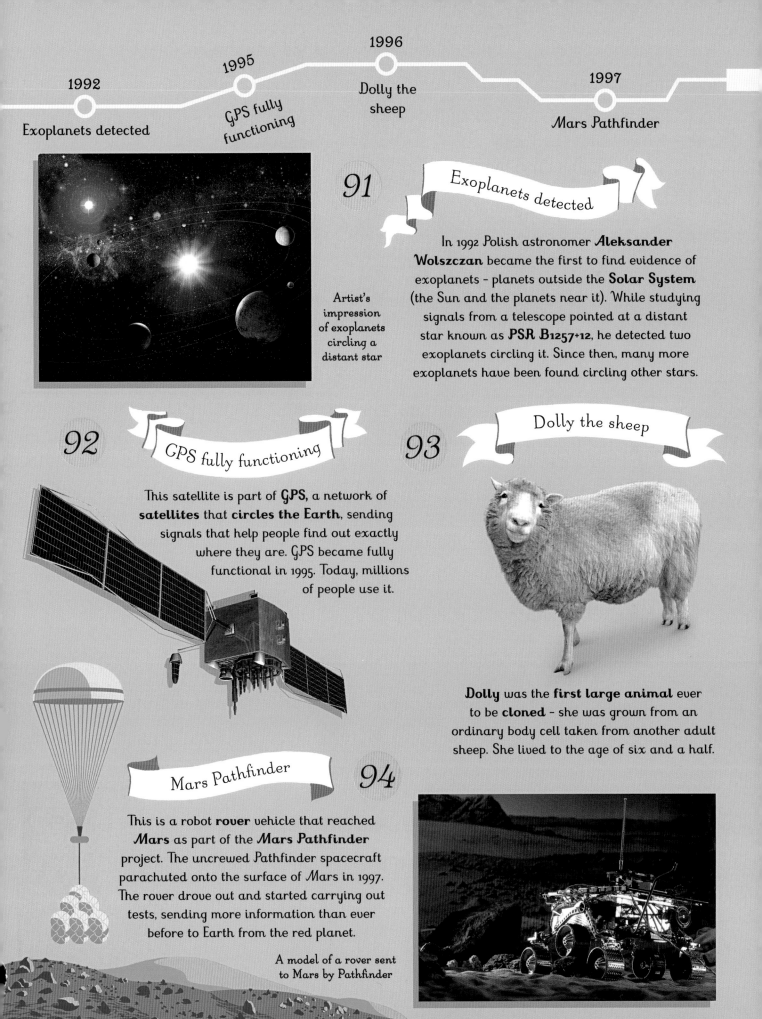

95 — Human Genome Project

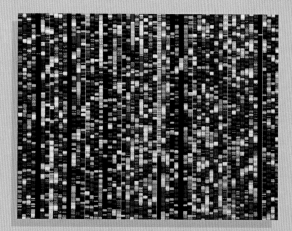

This is a screenshot of gene information collected as part of the **Human Genome Project**. Completed in 2001, it created a **list of all the genes** in human beings. It's a vast amount of information. If you printed out the entire genome, it would stretch 3,000km (almost 2,000 miles).

96 — Pluto becomes a dwarf

Pluto, shown here, used to be considered the ninth planet in the **Solar System**, until it was downgraded to **dwarf planet** status in 2006. Discovered in 1930 by American astronomer **Clyde Tombaugh** it was announced with great excitement as the ninth planet. But later research showed that Pluto was in fact much smaller than the moons of several other planets in the Solar System, so Pluto was reclassified.

97 — Artificial life

The first artificial bacterium

The world's first **living cell** containing entirely **man-made DNA** was created by American scientist **Craig Venter** and his team. They constructed some DNA in a lab, then removed the natural DNA from a **bacterium** (a tiny living organism) and injected the artificial DNA. The bacterium stayed alive and made copies of itself in a completely normal way.

2001 — Human Genome Project

2006 — Pluto becomes a dwarf

2010 — Artificial life

2012 — Higgs boson

98 Higgs boson

This diagram shows the trace (in red) of a minute **particle** known as a **Higgs boson**. Scientists in the 1960s predicted it existed, but they couldn't prove it. In 2012 the Higgs boson was detected using a vast machine known as a **particle accelerator**, run by the European research organization CERN. Scientists continue to research the Higgs boson and other tiny particles, to help them understand more about how the **Universe** works.

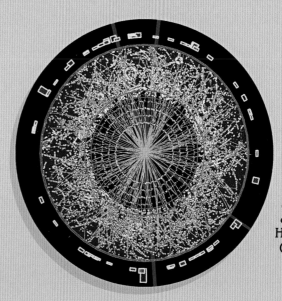

Image of a particle accelerator detecting a Higgs boson (in red)

Coral damaged by rising sea temperatures

99 Global climate change

Scientists all over the world investigated **sea temperature changes**, and other **changes in long-term weather patterns**, that put plants and animals at risk. Many argued these changes were caused by **human actions**, such as burning coal and gas. In 2013 the Intergovernmental Panel on Climate Change confirmed 'it is extremely likely that human influence has been the dominant cause'.

100 Black holes detected

In 2015, physicists found the first scientific proof of the existence of **black holes** – parts of space where **gravity** is so strong, it pulls everything inward and inward. The proof came when scientists detected **gravitational waves** caused by two black holes as they joined together. This artwork shows what this might look like.

2001 – 2015

2013
Global climate change

2015
Black holes detected

Index

Acknowledgements

Every effort has been made to trace and acknowledge ownership of copyright. If any rights have been omitted, the publishers offer to rectify this in any future editions following notification. The publishers are grateful to the following individuals and organizations for their permission to reproduce material on the following pages:

COVER tl © Science Photo Library/Alamy Stock Photo; mr © Granger Historical Picture Archive/Alamy Stock Photo; bl © SSPL/Getty Images.
PAGES 2-3 p2 ml © Denmark, Kopenhagen, Nationalmuseet, Oar from Ulkestrup Lyng/De Agostini Picture Library/Bridgeman Images; mr © Museum of London; bl © DEA/A. Dagli Orti/De Agostini/Getty Images; p3 tl © RMN-Grand Palais (musée du Louvre) / Christophe Chavan; tr © Paul Bevitt/Alamy Stock Photo; m © Art Collection 2/Alamy Stock Photo; br © World History Archive/Alamy Stock Photo.
PAGES 4-5 p4 tl © DEA Picture Library/De Agostini/Getty Images; tr © The Schøyen Collection MS 2192, Oslo and London; mr © dpa picture alliance archive/Alamy Stock Photo; br With thanks to Wulflund, manufacturer of historical reproductions, www.wulflund.com; p5 tl © DEA/A. Dagli Orti/De Agostini/Getty Images; mr © World History Archive/Alamy Stock Photo; bl © World History Archive/Alamy Stock Photo.
PAGE 6-7 p6 tl © Ancient Art and Architecture/Alamy Stock Photo; mr © Paul Fearn/Alamy Stock Photo; bl © National Archaeological Museum, Athens, Greece/Pictures from History/Bridgeman Images; p7 tr © Stan Sherer, www.stansherer.com; ml © www.kotsanas.com, Kostas Kotsanas, Ancient Greek Technology - The inventions of the ancient Greeks, p. 31; br © Ancient Art and Architecture Collection Ltd./Bridgeman Images.
PAGES 8-9 p8 tl © BnF, Dist. RMN-Grand Palais / image BnF; ml © Sheila Terry/ Science Photo Library; br © Inv.47632. © Museum of the History of Science, University of Oxford; p9 tl © SSPL/Getty Images; tr © DeAgostini/Getty Images; ml © Photo 12/Alamy Stock Photo; br © Prawns/Alamy Stock Photo.
PAGES 10-11 p10 tl © Universal Images Group North America LLC/Alamy Stock Photo; ml © British Library, London, UK/© British Library Board. All Rights Reserved/Bridgeman Images; m © The human anatomy/British Library, London, UK/© British Library Board. All Rights Reserved/Bridgeman Images; br Rivet glasses from Battle Abbey, Hastings, UK, with thanks to English Heritage; p11 tr © Mondadori portfolio/Electa/Paolo e Federico Manusardi/Bridgeman Images; ml © British Library, London, UK / © British Library Board. All Rights Reserved/Bridgeman Images; br © Universitatsbibliothek, Gottingen, Germany/Bildarchiv Steffens/Bridgeman Images.
PAGES 12-13 p12 tl © British Library, London, UK/© British Library Board. All Rights Reserved/Bridgeman Images; tr © The Granger Collection/Alamy Stock Photo; bl © Museo della Specola Universita di Bologna Dipartimento di Astronomia, Bologna, Italy/De Agostini Picture Library/Bridgeman Images; p13 tr © Granger Historical Picture Archive/Alamy Stock Photo; ml © National Portrait Gallery, London, UK/Bridgeman Images; bm © Natural History Museum, London/ Science Photo Library.
PAGES 14-15 p14 tr © Granger/Bridgeman Images; ml © Granger Historical Picture Archive/Alamy Stock Photo; br © Dorling Kindersley/UIG/Science Photo Library; p15 ml © Science History Images/Alamy Stock Photo; mr © Science History Images/Alamy Stock Photo.
PAGES 16-17 p16 tl © Museo Explorazione Civico Treviglio; bl © The Royal Institution, London, UK/Bridgeman Images; br © Science Museum/Science & Society Picture Library -- All rights reserved.; p17 ml © Oxford University Images/ Science Photo Library; tr © SSPL/Getty Images; bl © Edinburgh University Library, Scotland/With kind permission of the University of Edinburgh/Bridgeman Images; br © National Media Museum, Bradford, West Yorkshire/Bridgeman Images.
Pages 18-19 p18 tr © Cambridge University Library (DAR121, P 36); ml © Middle Temple Library/ Science Photo Library; br © Chronicle/Alamy Stock Photo; p19 ml © Charles D. Winters/ Science Photo Library; tr © Peter Horress/Alamy Stock Photo; br © © Science Museum / Science & Society Picture Library -- All rights reserved.; bl © VDWI Automotive/Alamy Stock Photo.
PAGES 20-21 p20 tl © World History Archive/Alamy Stock Photo; ml © Science Museum / Science & Society Picture Library -- All rights reserved.; br © Jean-Loup Charmet/ Science Photo Library; p21 tl © Dorling Kindersley/UIG/ Science Photo Library; tr © SSPL/Getty Images; bl © Claus Lunau/ Science Photo Library; br © incamerastock/Alamy Stock Photo.
PAGES 22-23 p22 tl © World History Archive/Alamy Stock Photo; mr © NASA/ Science Photo Library; bl © Science Museum/Science & Society Picture Library -- All rights reserved.; p23 tl © St. Mary's Hospital Medical School/ Science Photo Library; tr © Science Museum/Science & Society Picture Library -- All rights reserved.; bl Steve Nichols/Alamy Stock Photo; br © US Department of Energy.
PAGES 24-25 p24 tl © sciencephotos/Alamy Stock Photo; mr © Stephen Sweet/Alamy Stock Photo; bl © Andrew Burton/Getty Images; p25 tl © ITAR-TASS News Agency/Alamy Stock Photo; tr © Photo by Alfred Eisenstaedt/The LIFE Picture Collection/Getty Images; mr © Science Photo Library; bl © Pictorial Press Ltd/Alamy Stock Photo.
PAGES 26-27 p27 tr © Courtesy of FONAR Corporation; ml © Photo by Wendy Stone/Corbis via Getty Images; bl © Science Photo Library/Alamy Stock Photo; p27 tr © Laguna Design/ Science Photo Library; ml Photo © Associated Newspapers Ltd.; ml Newspaper page: © Granger Historical Picture Archive/Alamy Stock Photo; br © Science Photo Library/Alamy Stock Photo.
PAGES 28-29 p28 ml © SSPL/Getty Images; mr © 1990-2018 CERN (License: CC-BY-SA-4.0), Photograph: Patrice Loïez, http://cds.cern.ch/record/42413?ln=en; br © NASA/ESA/STSCI/ J. Hester & P.Scowen, ASU/Science Photo Library; p29 tl © Claus Lunau/ Science Photo Library; ml © Friedrich Saurer/Alamy Stock Photo; mr © Trinity Mirror/Mirrorpix/Alamy Stock Photo; br © RGB Ventures/SuperStock/Alamy Stock Photo.
PAGES 30-31 p30 tr © David Parker/ Science Photo Library; ml © Friederich Saurer/ Science Photo Library; br © Thomas Deerinck, NCMIR/ Science Photo Library; p31 tr © Atlas Collaboration/CERN/ Science Photo Library; ml © Georgette Douwma/ Science Photo Library; br © LIGO/Caltech/MIT/Sonoma State (Aurore Simonnet)/ Science Photo Library.

With thanks to Ruth King   Managing designer: Stephen Moncrieff

First published in 2018 by Usborne Publishing Ltd, Usborne House, 83-85 Saffron Hill, London EC1N 8RT, England. www.usborne.com